D0493079

Countries Around the World

Israel

Claire Throp

www.raintreepublishers.co.uk
Visit our website to find out more information about Raintree books.

To order:
Phone 0845 6044371
Fax +44 (0) 1865 312263
Email myorders@raintreepublishers.co.uk

Customers from outside the UK please telephone +44 1865 312262

Raintree is an imprint of Capstone Global Library Limited, a company incorporated in England and Wales having its registered office at 7 Pilgrim Street, London, EC4V 6LB – Registered company number: 6695582

Edited by Catherine Veitch and Charlotte Guillain
Designed by Steve Mead
Original illustrations © Capstone Global Library Ltd 2012
Illustrated by Oxford Designers & Illustrators
Picture research by Hannah Taylor
Originated by Capstone Global Library Ltd
Printed in China by CTPS

ISBN 978 1 406 23535 7
15 14 13 12 11
10 9 8 7 6 5 4 3 2 1

British Library Cataloguing in Publication Data
Throp, Claire.
Israel. -- (Countries around the world)
956.9'4054-dc22
A full catalogue record for this book is available from the British Library.

Acknowledgements
We would like to thank the following for permission to reproduce photographs: Alamy Images pp. 25 (© Alex Segre), 28 (© Israel Images), 34 (© M.Sobreira); Corbis pp. 7 (The Gallery Collection), 11 (Thomas Hartwell), 12 (Reuters/Paul Hanna), 13 (EPA/MICHAEL REYNOLDS), 16 (EPA/JIM HOLLANDER), 27 (EPA/JIM HOLLANDER), 31 (Hanan Isachar/AWL Images Ltd), 39 (Bettmann); Dreamstime p. 18 (© Smellme); Getty Images pp. 8 (AFP), 30 (AFP); Istockphoto pp. 20 (© kavram), 21 (© nitsan avivi), 22 (© Elena Zapassky); Shutterstock pp. 5 (© Yevgenia Gorbulsky), 14 (© Roman Sigaev), 19 (© hagit berkovich), 24 (© NEO), 29 (© Dmitry Pistrov), 33 (© bonchan), 35 (© Ryan Rodrick Beiler), 37 (© AlexGul).

Cover photograph of a Jewish person praying at the Wailing Wall, Jerusalem, Israel, reproduced with permission of Photolibrary (Imagebroker.net/ Fabian von Poser).

Every effort has been made to contact copyright holders of material reproduced in this book. Any omissions will be rectified in subsequent printings if notice is given to the publisher.

The author and publishers would like to thank Dr Colin Shindler and Marta Segal Block for their invaluable assistance in the preparation of this book.

Contents

Introducing Israel 4
History: the fight for a Jewish state 6
Regions and resources: a diverse country 14
Wildlife: nature and water 18
Infrastructure: parliamentary democracy 22
Culture: food, music, and sport 28
Israel today 34
Fact file 36
Timeline 40
Glossary 42
Find out more 44
Topic tools 46
Index 48

Some words in the book are in bold, **like this**. You can find out what they mean by looking in the glossary.

Introducing Israel

When you think of Israel what comes to mind? Famous places, such as the Western Wall, Bethlehem, and the Dead Sea? The country's food or range of different environments and wildlife? Or the conflict with the Palestinians? Israel is famous for these things and more.

Israel is in the Middle East, situated at the meeting point of three continents – Europe, Africa, and Asia. It is about the same size as Wales, with a population of around 7.4 million. Israel is one of the better-off countries in the Middle East. This is due to its large number of high-tech industries and **trade** links with Europe and the United States. Israel is bordered by Lebanon, Syria, Egypt, Jordan, and the Mediterranean Sea.

Religion

Israel is important for three separate religions because there are holy sites for Jewish, Muslim, and Christian people in the capital city, Jerusalem. This is part of the reason for the ongoing troubles in the region.

A modern state

Israel is a young country but the Jewish people have been linked to the area for thousands of years. Israel now is a place that Jews call home. Palestinians, however, believe the region is their home, too. Palestinians are the non-Jewish people who lived in the land that was Israel, before Israel was formed. This situation has led to conflict.

How to say...

The two main languages in Israel are Hebrew and Arabic.
Both languages are written in alphabets that are different from English.

	Hebrew	**Arabic**
hello	*shalom* (sha-lom)	*ahlan* (ahh-lan)
see you later	*lehitra'ot* (le-hit-ra-ot)	*ila-liqaa* (illa-liqaa)

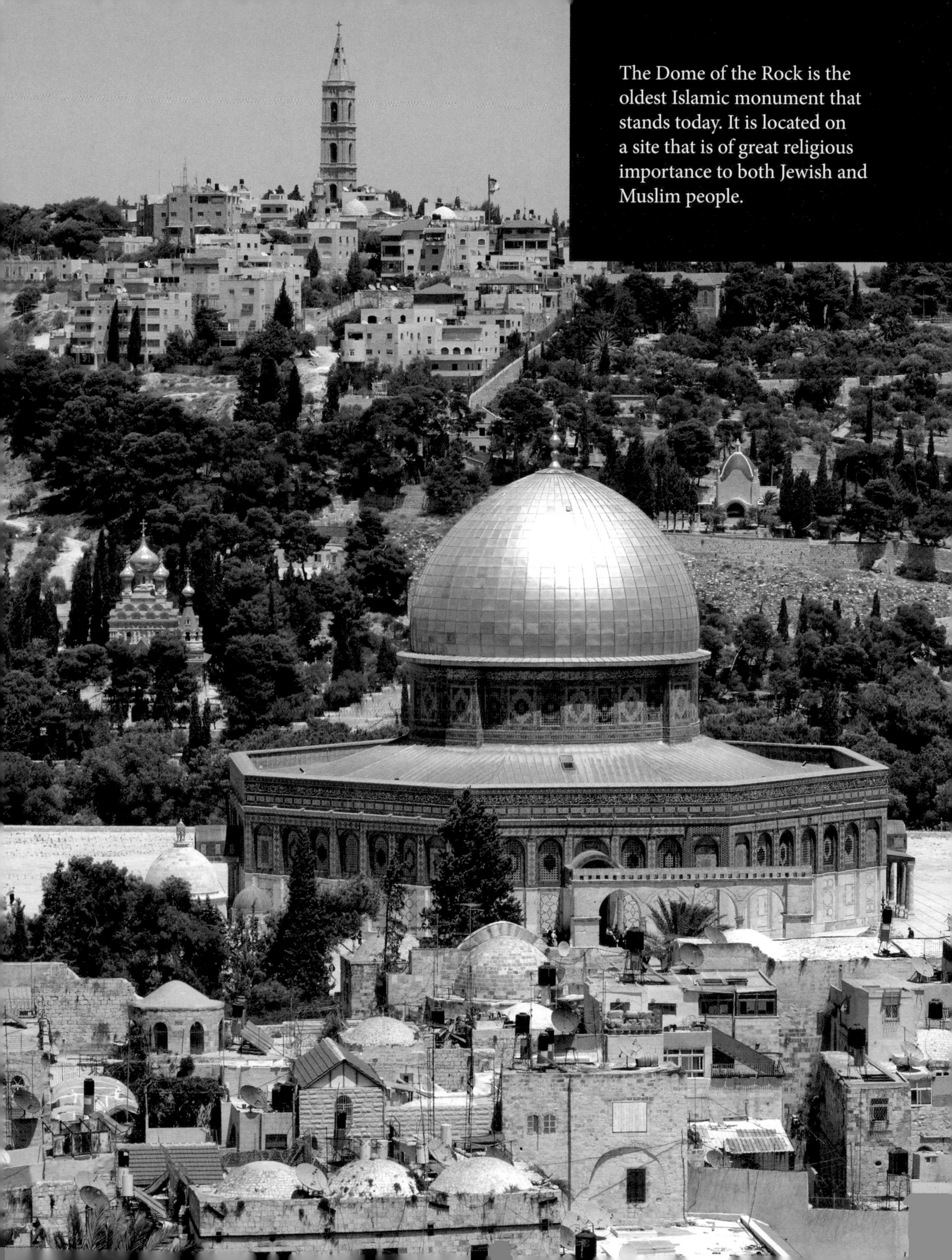

The Dome of the Rock is the oldest Islamic monument that stands today. It is located on a site that is of great religious importance to both Jewish and Muslim people.

History: the fight for a Jewish state

Jewish people lived in the area that is now Israel from before 1250 BC until the Bar-Kokhba revolt of AD 135 when they were forced out of their country by the Romans. Other invasions followed, by the Byzantines, the Muslim Arabs, the European Christians, and the Ottoman Turks. Most Jews were scattered around the world.

The British mandate

In 1897, Theodor Herzl formed the **Zionist** movement, which said that Jews should have their own country in ancient Israel. After the Balfour Declaration made by the British government in 1917, thousands of Jews began to move to the area that was once ancient Israel. This declaration promised a national home for the Jewish people, providing it did not affect the rights of the local, non-Jewish population.

The British and French were given **mandates** to rule the area by the **League of Nations**. From 1921, the British divided their area into Palestine, Transjordan, and Iraq. The Zionist Organization was chosen to represent Jewish people in Palestine. The Palestinian Arabs became worried about losing control of their lands as more and more Jews arrived.

The Holocaust

After Adolf Hitler became German leader in 1933, Jews in Germany, and then Jews in Nazi-controlled Europe, lost their rights, their businesses, and their homes. Nazi Germany tried to kill all European Jews during World War II (1939–45). They were sent to **concentration camps** and killed in **gas chambers**. Six million Jews died in the Holocaust – a third of all Jews in the world. After the State of Israel was created, many surviving European Jews went to live in Israel.

This painting shows an event that happened in AD 70. Roman troops are destroying the Second Temple in Jerusalem.

Security

In 2002, Israel built a security barrier around parts of the West Bank, blocking access to Jerusalem and parts of Israel. Israel said this was to secure their country from Palestinian attacks. Palestinians thought it was a way of gaining more of their land. The United States proposed a "Road Map" for peace in 2003. Israelis were to stop building settlements in land that they occupied militarily, and Palestinians had to stop their violence. Neither of these demands was met, however.

Big changes

In August 2005, Ariel Sharon, prime minister and leader of the Likud, ordered the evacuation of 21 Israeli settlements in the Gaza Strip and the northern West Bank. The Gaza Strip was now entirely under Palestinian control. In November, he resigned as head of Likud and formed a new political party called Kadima. Kadima won the 2006 election. The 2006 election in the Palestinian Authority was won by Hamas. Hamas supporters had introduced suicide bombing, did not recognize Israel, and wished to replace Israel with a Palestinian state.

In 2005, not every Israeli living in the Gaza settlements wanted to leave. Some had to be forced from their homes by soldiers.

Peace talks

Yet more peace talks began in 2007 and went well until December 2008. Then Israel attacked Gaza and talks were suspended. Israel said the attacks were in response to Palestinian rocket fire. However, other countries criticized Israel as far more Palestinians than Israelis were killed. In September 2010, peace talks were finally restarted. Israeli Prime Minister, Benjamin Netanyahu, and Palestinian leader, Mahmoud Abbas, met in Washington D.C., USA.

Netanyahu, Abbas, and Barack Obama the US President, were photographed as peace talks began again in September 2010.

Regions and resources: a diverse country

There are four main geographical areas in Israel: the coastal plain, rolling hills and mountains, a **rift valley**, and desert.

Rivers and seas

The River Jordan flows through the rift valley along the east of the country and into the Dead Sea. It is a major water source for Israel, Jordan, Syria, and Lebanon. There are Arab and Jewish **settlements** along the river, including the Hula Valley and the oldest **kibbutz** in Israel, Degania. The Dead Sea is a lake rather than a sea and is famous for its high levels of salt. Lake Tiberias in the north is also known as the Sea of Galilee. It is the largest freshwater lake in Israel.

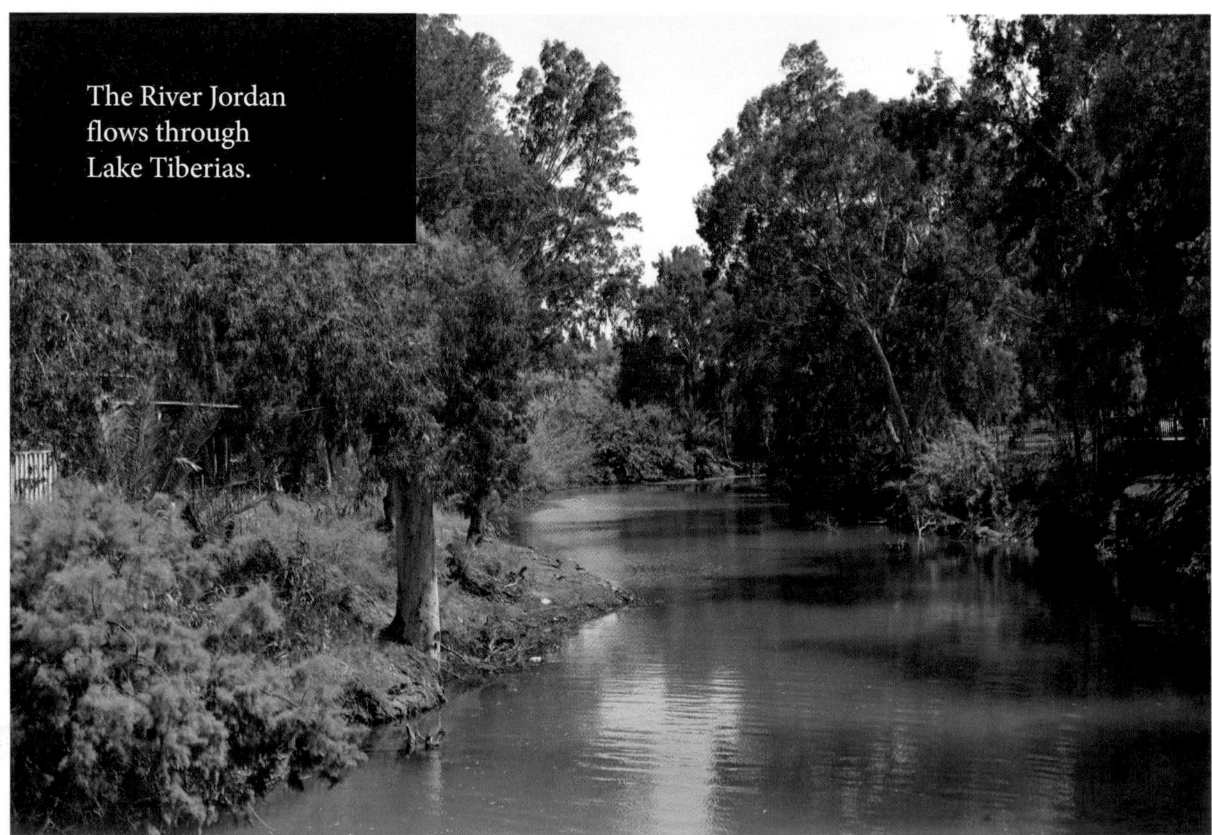

The River Jordan flows through Lake Tiberias.

Mountains and desert

Israel's highest mountain is Mount Meron in Galilee. It is about 1,208 metres (3,963 feet) high. The Negev Desert in the south takes up 62 per cent of Israel's land. A mountain range runs along the north of the Negev. Mount Ramon is the highest peak in the range at 1,035 metres (3,395 feet).

Natural disasters

Israel is in an active earthquake zone although it has been several hundred years since the last major earthquake. Flash floods can also occur.

Climate

Along the Mediterranean coast, Israel is generally hot, humid, and sunny, with a mild and wet winter from November to April. The north and east are less humid in the summer and have quite cold winters. The desert is nearly always hot and dry.

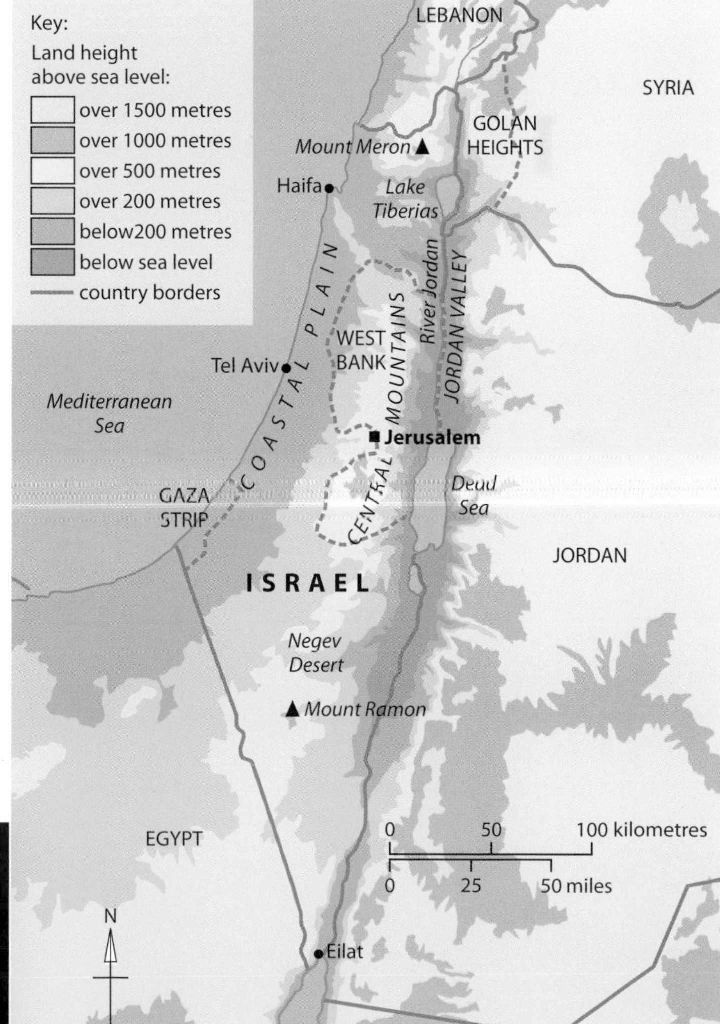

This map shows the physical features of Israel.

The economy

Israel was once a poor country but now has a standard of living similar to that of Western Europe. Israel was not badly affected by the global economic crisis that began in 2008. This was partly because the government had kept a tight control on the banking system in the years leading up to the crisis.

Daily life

Kibbutzim are farms that are jointly owned by the people who live there. Each farm is called a kibbutz. Everything is shared on a kibbutz, including work, decision-making, looking after children, food, and buildings. Today, products such as electrical goods are produced there, as well as agriculture. Moshavim are similar to kibbutzim but the people who live there have more independence. Families live and work separately but get together to sell their produce.

These workers are sorting Merlot grapes on a kibbutz in Israel. The grapes will be made into wine.

Resources and trade

There are few natural **resources** in Israel. Its people have worked hard to develop the land for agriculture, despite a lack of water and much of the land being desert. The **immigration** of skilled workers has helped to improve Israel's industrial sector. Israel has strong links with the United States. US aid is very important for Israel's **economy**, although much is spent on the military. Israel's other main trading partner is the European Union.

Jobs

There are about 4,000 technology companies in Israel. Manufacturing is also important, as the country produces machinery such as metal-cutting tools. Tourism has at times been affected by the violence in the country. In 2010, over three million tourists visited the country. Israel provides most of its own food, but agriculture is still a fairly small part of the economy. Palestinians are generally less well off than Israelis because they are often unable to get jobs in Israel. It is thought that poverty runs at about 50 per cent among Palestinians.

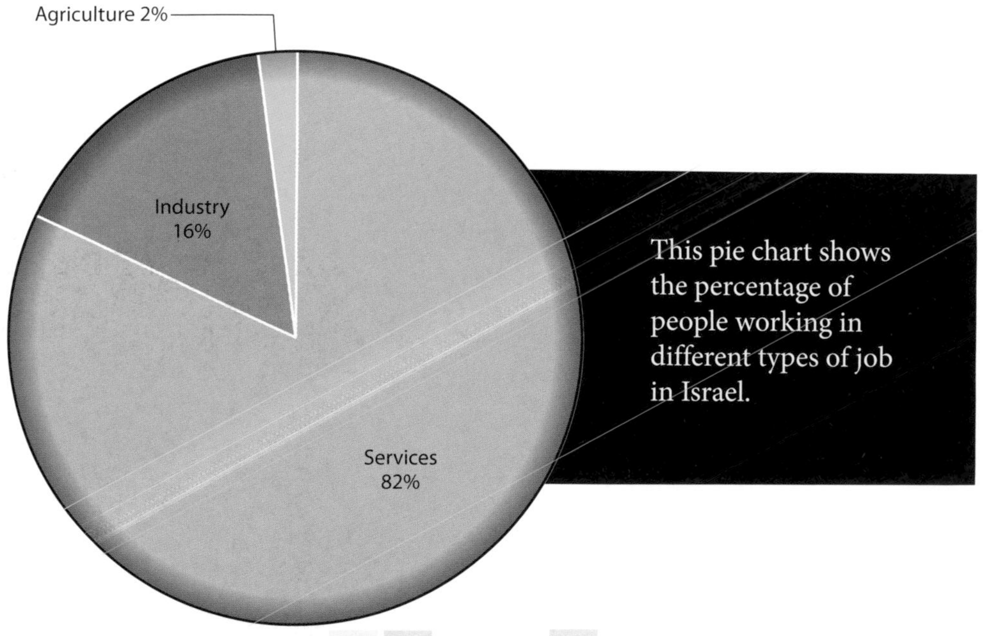

This pie chart shows the percentage of people working in different types of job in Israel.

Wildlife: nature and water

The eastern edge of Israel is part of the migration route of hundreds of bird **species**. Pelicans and cranes can be seen in places such as Eilat and the Hula Valley. Rare species such as griffon vultures and spotted eagles live in Israel's wildlife reserves.

YOUNG PEOPLE

"Migrating birds know no boundaries" is an educational programme set up by the International Center for the Study of Bird Migration in Tel Aviv. More than 300 schools in Israel, 30 in the Palestine Authority, and 30 in Jordan take part in research and education projects. The programme helps to bring children from different areas together.

Israel is home to the highly endangered griffon vulture.

Hai Bar

Hai Bar, which means "wildlife", is an organization that aims to protect the country's **endangered** animals and to reintroduce others. Some animals have been bred in captivity (enclosed places such as zoos) and released into the wild. As a result, animals such as the fennec fox and the desert hedgehog are now lower down on the endangered animal lists.

Scorpions can be seen in the desert and Israel is one of the few places where green turtles nest. Snakes and lizards are also common.

Plants

Israel has nearly 3,000 plant species, including desert flowers such as irises in Gilboa reserve, and orchids near Jerusalem. Israel is also the only place where a tree called the Euphrates poplar still grows.

How to say...

	Hebrew	Arabic
fox	*shoual* (shoo-al)	*ta'lab* (ta'lab)
eagle	*nesher* (ne-sher)	*nasr* (nasr)
snake	*nakhash* (nah-khash)	*af'aa* (af'aa)

The fennec fox is a **conservation** success story.

Timna National Park contains some amazing rocks, including Solomon's pillars.

National parks

Israel has 65 national parks that cover 1,000 square kilometres (386 square miles). The parks are not always vast open spaces but can be castles, churches, and caves. There are also 150 nature reserves.

Water conservation

The dry climate means that water conservation is an important issue in Israel. A system of canals, tunnels, and pipelines takes water from Lake Tiberias to the rest of the country. Other projects include **desalination** of seawater. **Irrigation** is a way of watering land or crops in areas that do not get much rainfall. High-tech irrigation has been used to turn desert areas into farmland. Israel pioneered a system of drip irrigation, where narrow pipes with holes are used to drip water on to crops. The system is controlled by computer. Water wastage is only ten per cent but drip irrigation is expensive, so is only used on high-value crops, such as fruit, vegetables, and flowers.

Environmental issues

One of the results of Israel's water management systems is that less water reaches the Dead Sea. As well as this, some companies are **evaporating** Dead Sea water to use the salts in make-up and spa goods. This means that the Dead Sea is disappearing by about one metre (three feet) in depth every year.

Air pollution in Israel often reaches dangerous levels. Also, the huge increase in population in recent years has meant that much land has been taken over by housing and industry.

Agriculture has been made possible in Israel as a result of irrigation systems.

Infrastructure: parliamentary democracy

Israel is a **parliamentary democracy**. Citizens elect representatives, who then appoint high-level politicians. Everyone over 18 can vote. The **head of state** is an elected president, but he or she has no real power. The leader of the government is the **prime minister**. He or she is chosen by the president and party leaders. Israel's **parliament**, the Knesset, has 120 members.

The Palestinian Authority

In the West Bank and Gaza, the Palestinians have their own **political parties** and leaders. The **nationalist** Fatah party won the 2005 election for President of the Palestinian Authority. In 2006, the **Islamist** Hamas party won the election for the Legislative Council. Since 2007, Hamas has effectively ruled Gaza and Fatah has ruled the West Bank.

The Knesset is in Jerusalem.

Jerusalem

Until 1967, the city of Jerusalem was divided into West Jerusalem, controlled by Israel, and East Jerusalem, controlled by Jordan. Israel captured East Jerusalem in the 1967 war. Today, the Palestinians want East Jerusalem to be their capital. Israel currently claims that Jerusalem is their capital city. However, this has not been internationally recognized.

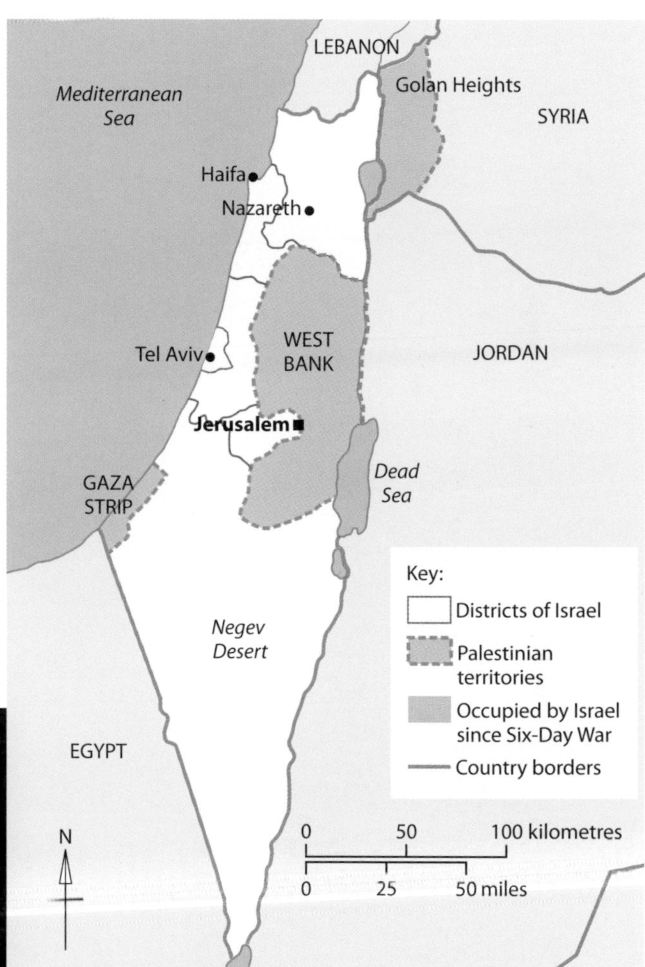

This map shows the six districts of Israel. They are divided into 15 sub-districts.

Daily life

The Hebrew language had not been spoken for many years when Eliezer Ben-Yehuda suggested bringing it back as a spoken language in 1879. Before this it was used only in prayer and studies. Modern Hebrew was accepted as one of three official languages (along with English and Arabic) in British-ruled Palestine in 1921. It was then established as the official language of Israel in 1948. Modern Hebrew is written from right to left using the 22 letters of the Hebrew alphabet.

The Israeli Defence Force

Israelis must do two or three years of **national service** and do basic reserve duty each year In the Israeli Defence Force (IDF). Their names are then kept on a list and they are called up to fight if and when necessary. However, many younger people do not like to be forced into national service and think Israel should have a professional army like other countries.

Daily life

Some people living in Israeli **settlements** in areas such as the West Bank live very dangerous lives. Palestinians do not like the Israeli settlements because they believe it shows Israelis will never move out. Settlers often keep a gun at home and travel to work in armoured buses. There are attacks made by Palestinians on settlers and sometimes by settlers on Palestinians.

Health

Israel has several internationally famous hospitals. Medical facilities in the country are often excellent and both free and private clinics are available. Health tourism is also becoming very popular. Spas based at hot springs or near the Dead Sea are visited by many tourists.

The health properties of the Dead Sea are well known. The mud is good for skin problems.

Media and technology

Many different newspapers, television channels, and radio stations reflect the different cultures in Israel. The Israel Broadcasting Authority provides television and radio channels and there are commercial and satellite channels available, too.

In 2008, 71.1 per cent of Israelis had computers at home and 90.8 per cent of those had an internet connection. Most cafes and hotels have internet connections too. Each household has an average of two mobile phones.

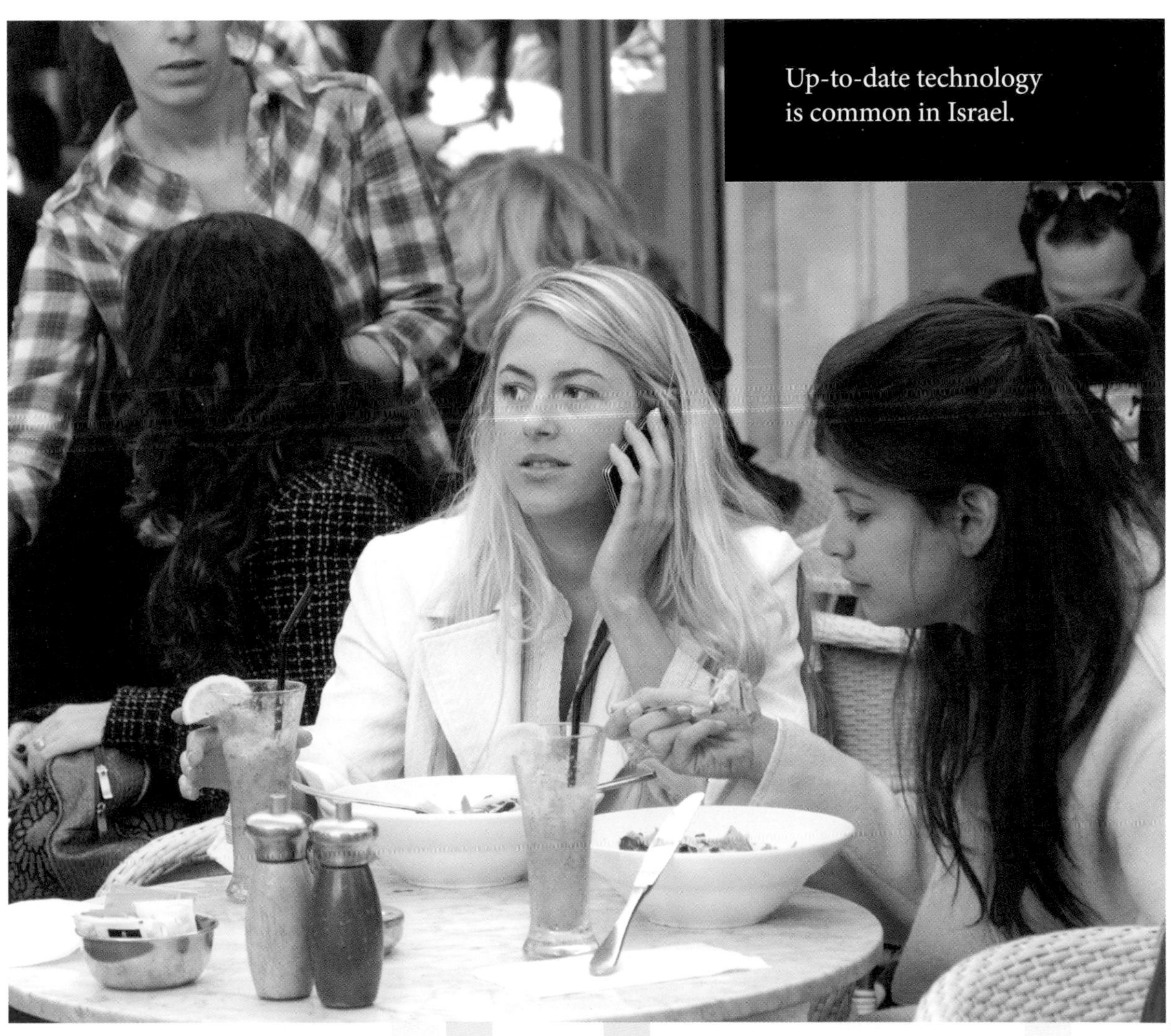

Up-to-date technology is common in Israel.

School life

Israeli children go to school from the age of 6 up to the age of 18. Schooling is free. Schools are divided into four types: state schools (where most children go); state religious schools (which focus on Judaism); Arab schools (which focus on Arab history and religion); and private schools (that charge fees). Each year a special topic of national importance, such as the environment, is closely studied.

Secondary education

Secondary education includes **vocational** schools such as technical, military, or agricultural schools. These prepare students for specific jobs. Other secondary schools teach standard subjects such as history and geography.

Higher education

There are world-famous universities in Israel that attract students from around the world. Many Israelis do not begin their studies until at least the age of 21 because of national service, which is three years for men and two for women.

Daily life

Palestinian children have often suffered during the Israel-Palestine conflict. Some have been killed, while others have been harshly treated by Israeli soldiers. Fighting affects schools and health centres. Money and materials have not been available to repair 82 per cent of the buildings, so schools have become overcrowded, unhygienic, and unsafe. Education standards for Palestinian children have been falling as a result.

YOUNG PEOPLE

The Re'ut Sadaka movement encourages Israeli Jews and Arabs aged 14 to 18 to meet and become friends. *Re'ut* means friendship in Hebrew and Arabic. Jews and Arabs tend to live in different areas and go to different schools. This movement aims to help young people to develop an understanding of each other's culture.

These Muslim and Jewish school children are at the Bible Lands Museum in Jerusalem. They are taking part in a programme that aims to bring together Jews and Muslims by focusing on their shared history.

Culture: food, music, and sport

Israelis love the Eurovision Song Contest, as well as *Mizrahi* (Eastern music sung in Hebrew), rock, and pop music. Palestinian rap is popular and focuses on issues such as the occupation of their land by the Israelis. There is a strong classical music tradition, partly as a result of European Jews bringing their love of classical music with them. The Israeli Philharmonic Orchestra is known worldwide.

Famous theatres can be found in Tel Aviv and Jerusalem. The Habima Theater in Tel Aviv is probably the most important and is considered the national theatre of Israel. Plays that comment on political issues are often as popular as the musicals brought in from the United Kingdom or the United States.

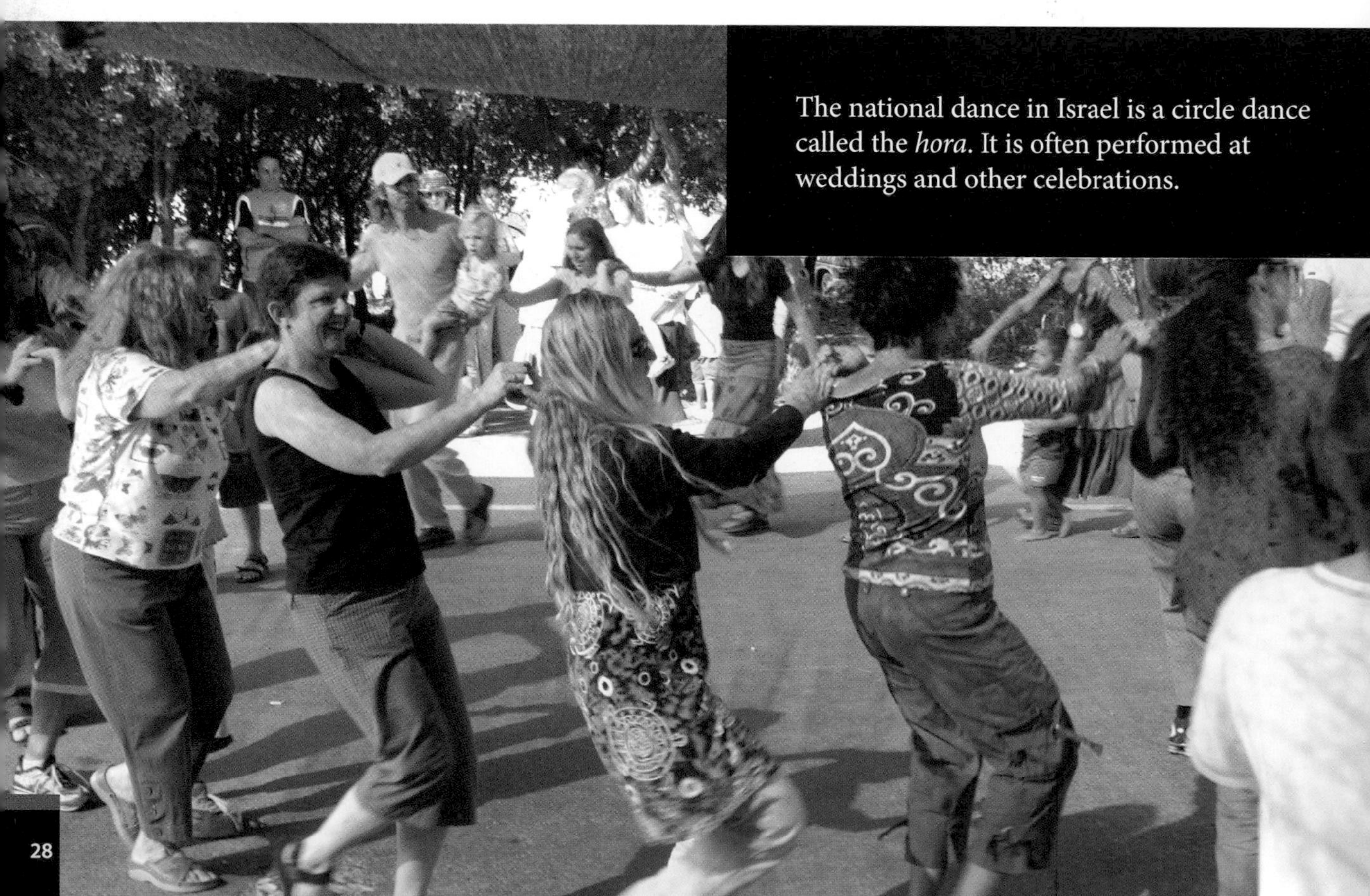

The national dance in Israel is a circle dance called the *hora*. It is often performed at weddings and other celebrations.

Literature

The International Jerusalem Book Fair is attended by people from more than 40 countries. People come to see who wins the celebrated Jerusalem Prize for Literature. Amos Oz, A. B. Yehoshua, and David Grossman are well-known Israeli writers. Palestinians such as Sahar Khalifeh have written about the hardships of Palestinian women's lives.

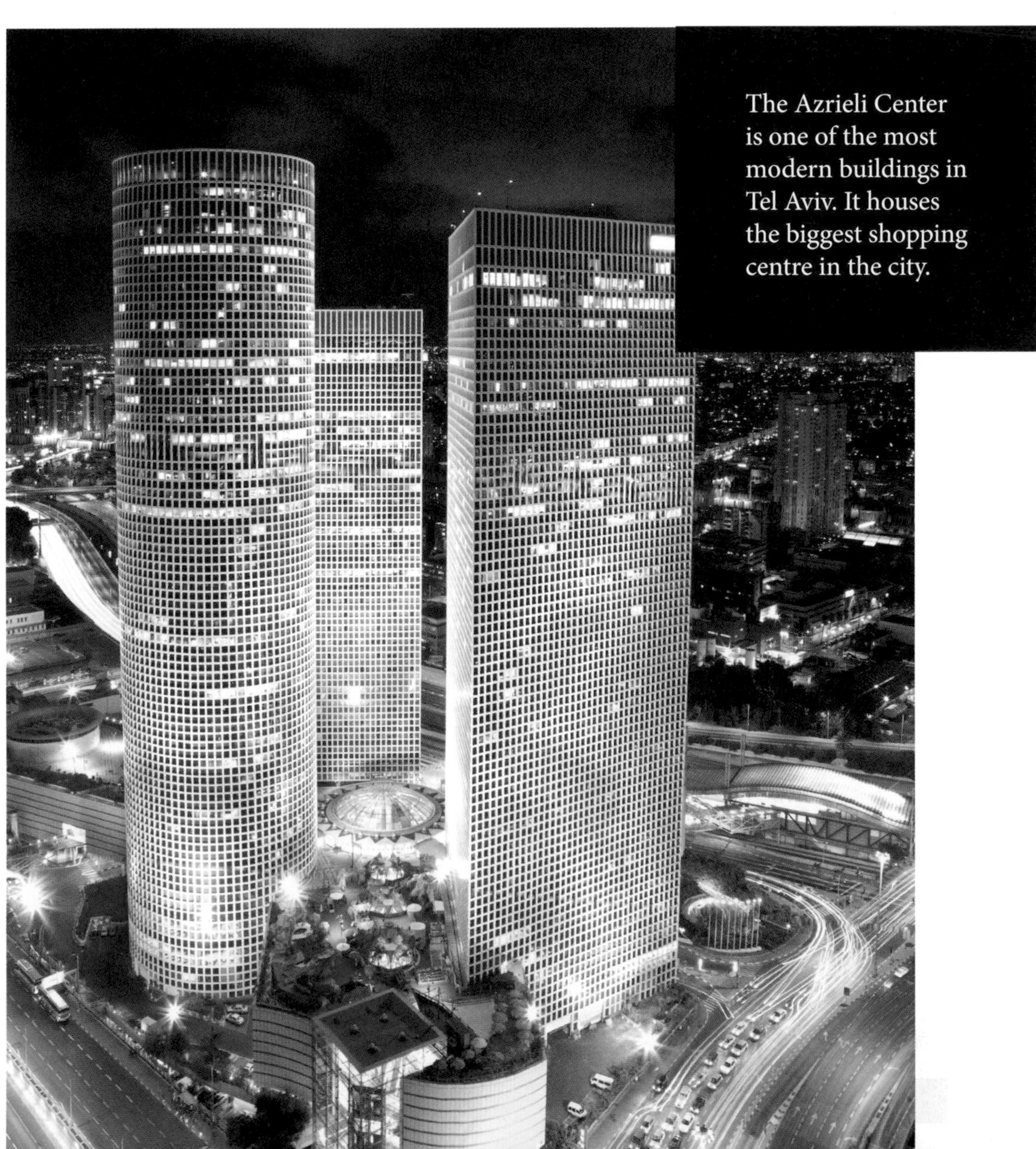

The Azrieli Center is one of the most modern buildings in Tel Aviv. It houses the biggest shopping centre in the city.

Film industry

Several Israeli films have been in the running for an Oscar (film award), such as *Waltz with Bashir* (2008). Haifa and Jerusalem hold international film festivals every year. The Steven Spielberg Film Archive in the Hebrew University of Jerusalem has the world's largest collection of Jewish and Israeli films.

Sport

Football and basketball are the most popular sports in Israel but mountain biking and other outdoor sports are also enjoyed. The Maccabiah Games, held in Israel every four years for Jewish sportspeople from around the world, are a major cultural event.

A dark day in Israeli sporting history took place in 1972. At the Olympics in Munich, Germany, two Israeli athletes were killed and nine others kidnapped by Palestinian **terrorists**. Israel's participation in the Olympics had been seen as a huge step towards repairing relations with Germany after the Holocaust, but things went horribly wrong. The terrorists demanded Palestinian prisoners be freed but Israel refused. By the end of the day, all 11 Israelis were killed in a shoot-out.

At the Beijing Olympic Games in 2008, Israel played China in the men's wheelchair basketball competition.

Women

Many women in Israel lead lives similar to Europeans, working and raising small families. The Women's Equal Rights law was passed in 1951. This gives women equality with men by law but sometimes religious views may counteract this. Women from **Orthodox** Jewish families often have a stricter, more traditional lifestyle. Many stay at home as they tend to have large families, although some may teach or work in an office.

YOUNG PEOPLE

Israeli families love camping, for example by the Sea of Galilee beaches. Those on the eastern coast are particularly popular with teenagers. They camp, swim, and have barbecues. Gan Hashlosha National Park (Sahne) is a popular spot for children to go swimming and have picnics. It has a natural pool fed by **aquifers** that is warm all year round.

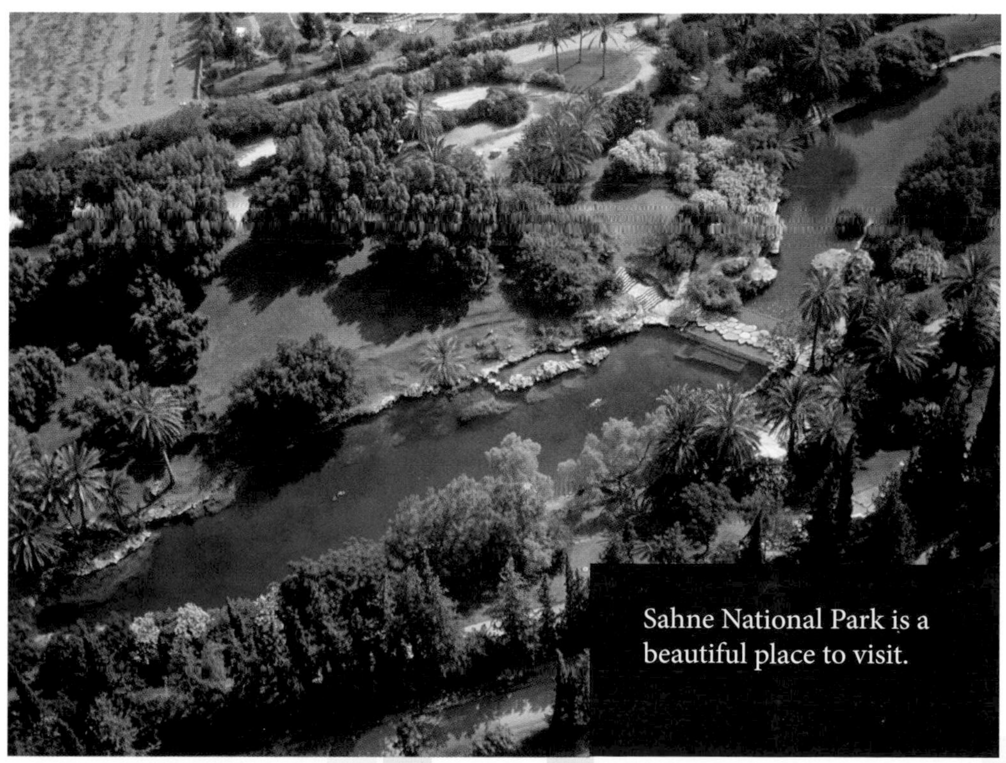

Sahne National Park is a beautiful place to visit.

Religion

More than three-quarters of Israel's population is Jewish. Most are not regular worshippers but there are many Orthodox Jews who observe the Jewish religion in every detail. Shabbat (Saturday) is a day of rest for Jewish people and in many places everything shuts. Some people avoid doing any work, travelling by car, or even answering the telephone on Shabbat.

Food and meals

Popular Israeli foods include olives, grapes, apricots, and other fruits as well as hummus, and falafel. One of the favourite meals is chicken soup with matzah meal dumplings, called matzah balls.

Israelis usually eat their main meal at noon when children are home from school. The evening meal consists of salads and dairy foods. Israelis often eat a large breakfast, which includes salad, cheese, olives, bread, and coffee.

There are some rules about food, called **Kosher** laws, that Jewish people are supposed to follow. For example, they are not allowed to eat pork, and meat and dairy foods cannot be stored or cooked together. The Palestinian territories are mainly Muslim and they, too, do not eat pork. Muslims are also not supposed to drink alcohol.

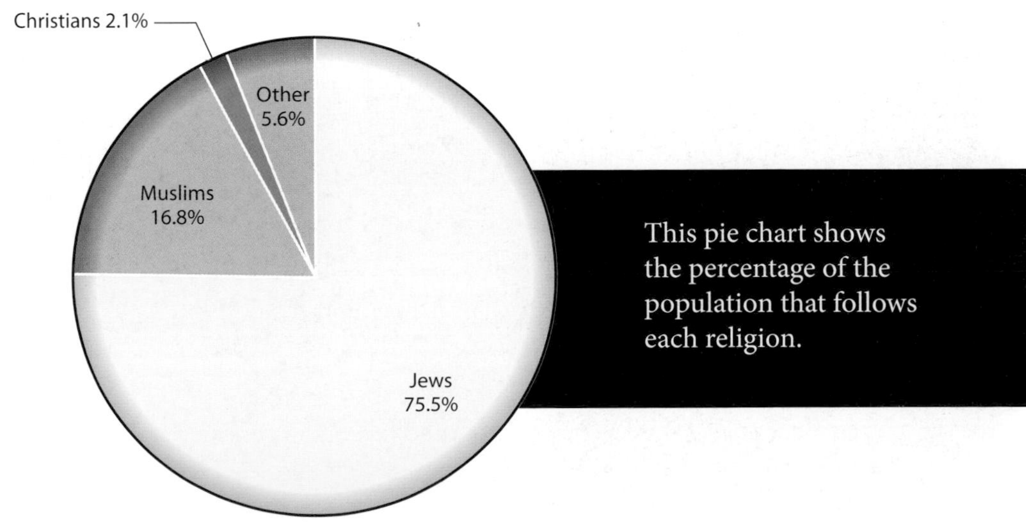

This pie chart shows the percentage of the population that follows each religion.

Falafel

Ask an adult to help you make this tasty snack.

Ingredients

- 400 gram tin of chickpeas
- 1 large onion, chopped
- 2 cloves of garlic, chopped
- 3 tablespoons of fresh parsley, chopped
- 1 teaspoon ground coriander
- 1 teaspoon cumin
- 2 tablespoons of flour
- Salt and pepper
- Sunflower or vegetable oil

What to do

1. Drain the chickpeas, and place them in a saucepan with fresh water, and bring to a boil. Allow to boil for 5 minutes, then simmer on low for about 10 minutes, so the chickpeas become a little softer.
2. Drain and allow to cool for 15 minutes.
3. Combine the chickpeas, onion, garlic, parsley, coriander, cumin, salt, and pepper in a medium-sized bowl.
4. Mash the ingredients together with a fork until they are a rough paste. Add the flour.
5. Mould the mixture into small balls, each one about the size of a ping-pong ball. Slightly flatten each ball.
6. Fry in about 8 centimetres (3 inches) of oil at a temperature of 180°C (350°F) until golden brown (for about 4 minutes). Remove with a slotted spoon and drain on kitchen roll. Serve hot or cold.

Israel today

Israel has come a long way since 1948. Its population has grown enormously. The **immigration** of skilled workers has helped the **economy** to develop. Tourism is increasing, despite fears about safety. The religious importance of Jerusalem means that pilgrims will always travel to Israel. Many Israelis are proud of the way they have built their country up from poor beginnings to a nation with living standards roughly equal to those in Western Europe.

It is true, however, that like many Western countries, there is a widening gap between rich and poor. Many Palestinian **refugees** still live in refugee camps in Arab countries (except in Jordan). There were at least four million of these refugees in 2010. This is just one of the many issues that Israelis and Arabs will need to address if the peace process is to end positively.

Hope for peace

At the end of 2010, peace talks were continuing. The hope is that eventually an Israeli state and a Palestinian state can exist side by side. Violence and **suicide bombers** may become a thing of the past. How long it will take to get there is impossible to know, but most people hope that peace comes soon.

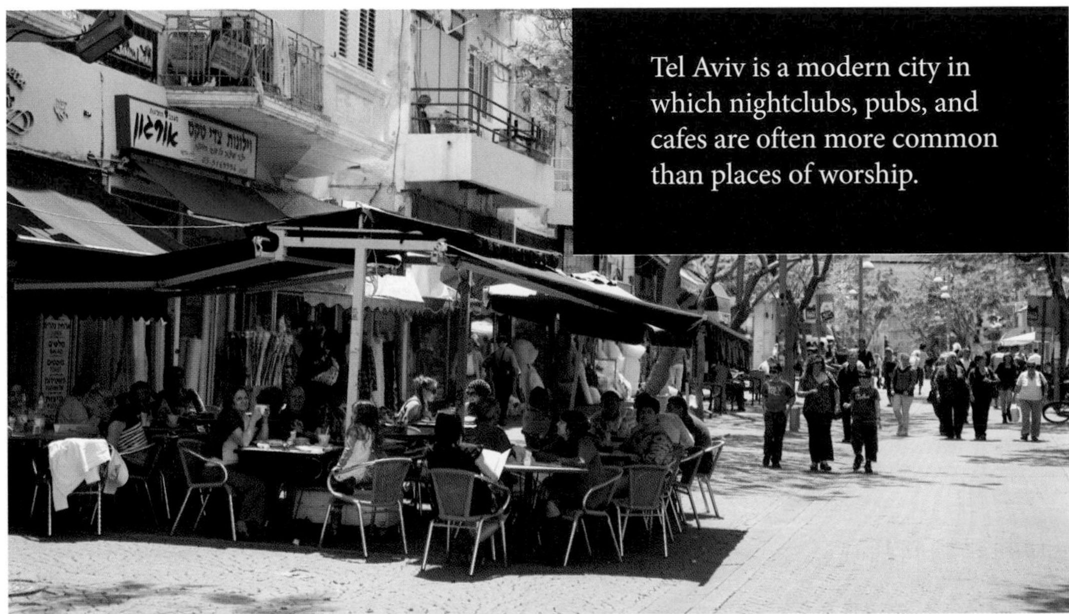

Tel Aviv is a modern city in which nightclubs, pubs, and cafes are often more common than places of worship.

The Western Wall is a place of **pilgrimage** for Jews. They write prayers on pieces of paper and stick them in gaps in the wall.

Fact file

Name:	State of Israel
Government:	**parliamentary democracy**
Area:	22,072 square kilometres (8,522 square miles), including Jerusalem and Golan
Bordering countries:	Lebanon; Syria; Jordan; Egypt
Capital:	Jerusalem (not internationally recognized)
Largest city:	Jerusalem
Population:	7.4 million (July 2010 est.)
Life expectancy at birth:	79 (men); 83 (women)
Languages:	Hebrew; Arabic
Currency:	1 New Israeli Shekel (ILS) = 100 new agorot
Religion:	Judaism and Islam with minority Christian
Longest river:	River Jordan at 360 kilometres (224 miles)
Highest point:	Mount Meron at 1,208 metres (3,963 feet)
Lowest point:	Dead Sea at 400 metres (1,312 feet) below sea level
Coastline:	273 kilometres (170 miles)
Imports:	military equipment; grain; fuels; rough diamonds
Exports:	computer software; cut diamonds; minerals; paper products; chemicals; military equipment; citrus fruits

Public holidays

Jewish people use the Jewish or Hebrew calendar for religious purposes. It is based on 12 lunar months (354 days) but with an extra month added every few years so that it matches the solar year (365 days). A Jewish holiday falls on the same day of every Jewish calendar year. This is why it appears in different months in the Gregorian calendar used by most of the Western world.

These Jewish public holidays fall in the following months:
February/March: Purim
March/April: Passover
April/May: Holocaust Memorial Day; National Memorial Day; Independence Day
May/June: Shavuot
July/August: Tisha B'Av
September: Rosh Hashanah
September/October: Yom Kippur; Sukkot; Simhat Torah
December: Hannukah

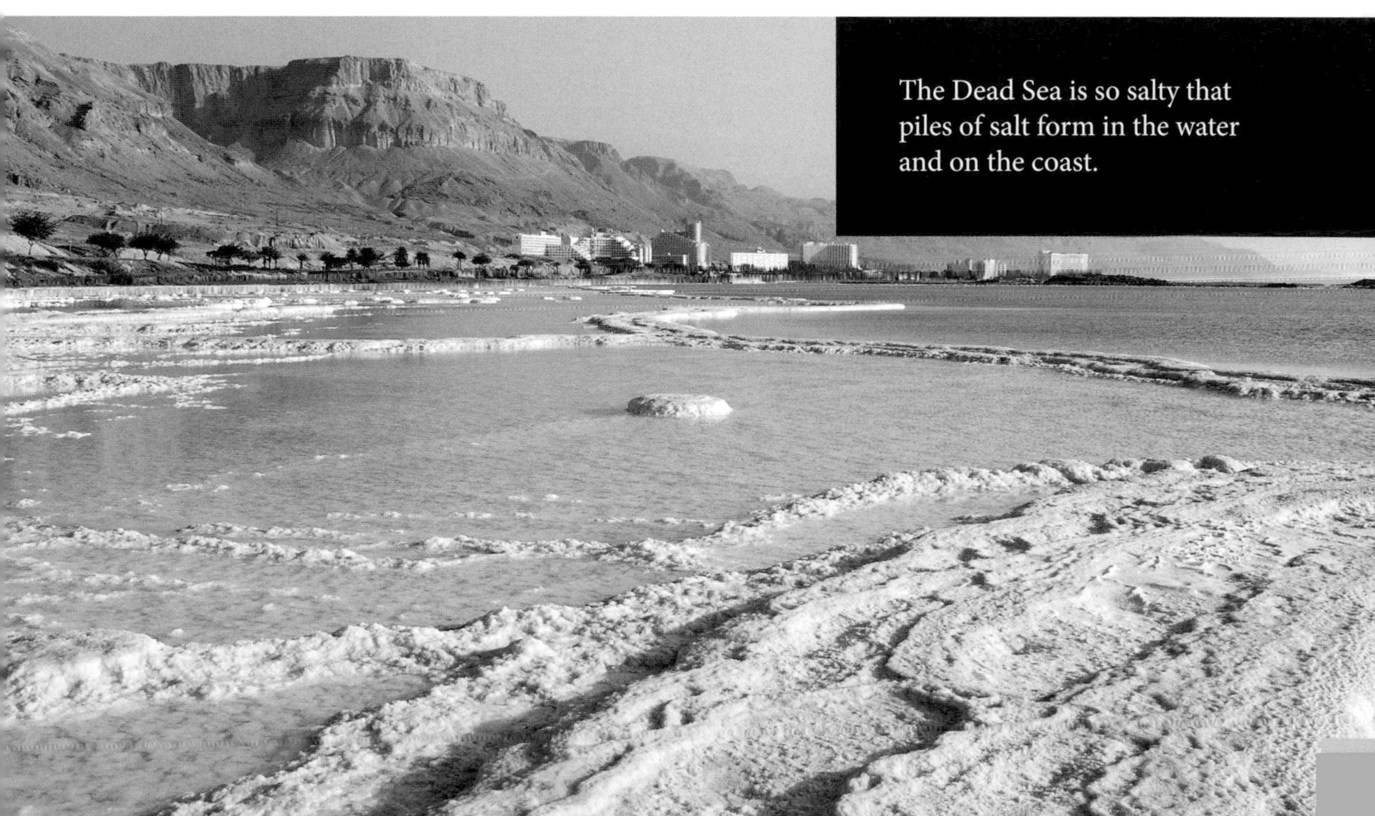

The Dead Sea is so salty that piles of salt form in the water and on the coast.

National anthem: *Hatikva* (The Hope)

As long as deep in the heart,
The soul of a Jew yearns,
And forward to the East
To Zion, an eye looks
Our hope will not be lost,
The hope of two thousand years,
To be a free nation in our land,
The land of Zion and Jerusalem.

How to say...

	Hebrew	
Monday	*yom sheni*	(yom-shey-nee)
Tuesday	*yom shlishi*	(yom-shlee-shee)
Wednesday	*yom revi'i*	(yom-re-vee-ee)
Thursday	*yom khamishi*	(yom-kha-mee-shee)
Friday	*yom shishi*	(yom-shee-shee)
Saturday	*shabbat*	(sha-bat)
Sunday	*yom rishon*	(yom ree-shon)

	Arabic	
Monday	*yom al-itneen*	(yawm al-itnayn)
Tuesday	*yom al-talaata*	(yawm al-talaata)
Wednesday	*yom al-arba'a*	(yawm al-arba'a)
Thursday	*yom al-khamees*	(yawm al-khamees)
Friday	*yom al-jum'a*	(yawm al-jum'a)
Saturday	*yom al-sabt*	(yawm al-sabt)
Sunday	*yom al-ahad*	(yawm al-ahad)

GOLDA MEIR (1898-1978)

Golda Meir was born in Kiev, Ukraine. She trained as a teacher in the United States but in her twenties she travelled to what would become Israel, to live on a **kibbutz**. She was active in politics for many years. At the age of 70, she became **prime minister** and led Israel during the Yom Kippur War of 1973. The war did not go well and she resigned a few months after the end of the war. She died of cancer in 1978.

Timeline

BC is short for "before Christ". BC is added after a date and means that the date occurred before the birth of Jesus Christ, for example, 450 BC.

AD is short for Anno Domini, which is Latin for "in the year of our Lord". AD is added before a date and means that the date occurred after the birth of Jesus Christ, for example, AD 720.

before 1250 BC	Jews first live in area now known as Israel
AD 66–70	First Jewish War against Romans
70	Jewish people forced out of Jerusalem by Titus and the Roman army, who destroy the Second Temple
135	Bar-Kokhba revolt
638	Arabs conquer Jerusalem
1099	Massacre of Jews by the Crusaders as they conquer Jerusalem
1897	Theodor Herzel forms the **Zionist** movement
1917	The Balfour Declaration says there will be a national home created for Jews in Palestine
1921	**League of Nations** gives **mandates** to Britain and France to rule area now known as Israel
1939–45	World War II sees the killing of six million Jews in what is known as the Holocaust
1947	British hand control of Palestine to the **United Nations**
1948	David Ben-Gurion proclaims independent State of Israel. Hebrew becomes the official language of Israel.
May 1948–Jan 1949	First Arab-Israeli war
1967	Six-Day War in which Israel occupies the West Bank, Gaza Strip, East Jerusalem, Golan Heights, and Sinai Peninsula
1972	Kidnapping and death of 11 Israeli staff and athletes at the Munich Olympics
1973	Yom Kippur War between Israel and Egypt

1978	Israel and Egypt agree peace
1980	Israel announces that Jerusalem is the capital of Israel
1982	Israel invades Lebanon
1987	First **Intifada** begins
1990s	Huge increase in Jewish **immigration** to Israel from states of the former Soviet Union
1993	Israel and Palestinians sign the Oslo Accords
1995	**Prime Minister** Yitzhak Rabin is killed by a Jewish **extremist**
2000	Israeli troops withdraw from Lebanon. The Second Intifada begins.
2002	Israel builds a wall around parts of the West Bank
2005	Ariel Sharon, the Likud Prime Minister, sets up a new party called Kadima; Israelis leave Gaza and four **settlements** in northern West Bank. Citizens who do not leave voluntarily are forced out.
2006	Hamas wins Palestinian Authority election
2006	Israel attacks Lebanon over kidnapping of Israeli soldier
2007	Hamas take over Gaza
2008	Peace talks break down as Israel launches attack on Gaza in response to what the Israelis say was Palestinian rocket fire
2010	Peace talks restart in Washington D.C., USA, under the guidance of the United States
2011	Hamas and Fatah begin talks

Glossary

aquifer underground lake of water

ceasefire agreement to stop fighting during a war

concentration camp place in which large numbers of people, often minorities such as Jews in World War II, are imprisoned. The camps are usually crowded with very basic facilities.

conservation looking after things such as animals or the environment to prevent them from being damaged or destroyed

desalination way of making sea water drinkable by removing the salt from it

economy to do with money and the industry and jobs in a country

endangered when animals or plants are seriously at risk of dying out

evaporate heat a liquid until it becomes a gas

extremist person who holds extreme political or religious views

gas chamber airtight room that can be filled with poisonous gas. Gas chambers were used by the Nazis in World War II to kill Jewish people.

head of state person who represents a country. Sometimes they are also the leader of the country.

immigration act of coming to live in a foreign country

Intifada Palestinian uprising against the Israeli occupation of the West Bank and Gaza Strip

irrigation way of watering land or crops in areas that do not get much rainfall

Islamist favouring an extreme form of Islam

kibbutz settlement – often a farm – in which people work and live together, sharing everything

Kosher set of rules for the way food must be prepared and eaten by Jewish people

League of Nations organization of countries set up to promote peace

mandate official order to do something

national service period of time that each person has to spend in the army

nationalist person who wants independence for their country

Orthodox conforming strictly to a set of traditions or religious beliefs

parliament ruling body of some countries; laws are made there

parliamentary democracy system of government in which citizens elect representatives, and these representatives, in turn, appoint high-level politicians such as the prime minister

pilgrimage journey to a place of particular interest, usually a religious place

political party group of people who believe in the same things. A political party is an organization that tries to gain power in the government.

prime minister head of a parliamentary government

refugee person who has been forced to leave their country because of war or persecution

resources means available for a country to develop, such as minerals and energy sources

rift valley steep-sided valley

right wing holding conservative values and not wanting change

settlement place where people set up a community

species type of animal, bird, or fish

stateless when a person is not recognized as a member of any country, which means they do not have the rights of a citizen

suicide bombers people who plan a bomb attack on other people or a place and who expect to die from the attack themselves

terrorist person who uses violence to achieve a political aim

trade buying and selling goods and services

United Nations (UN) organization of countries set up to promote peace. The United Nations took over from the League of Nations in 1945.

vocational relating to a particular job

Zionist relating to a movement with the aim to re-establish a Jewish nation

Find out more

Books

Changing World: Israel, Susie Hodge (Franklin Watts, 2008)

Countries in the News: Israel, Michael Gallagher (Franklin Watts, 2006)

Countries of the World: Israel, Emma Young (National Geographic, 2008)

Regions of the World: The Middle East and North Africa, Rob Bowden et al (Heinemann Library, 2008)

The Atlas of People and Places, Philip Steele (Franklin Watts, 2008)

The Middle East: Israel and Palestine, John King (Raintree, 2006)

Websites

www.israelemb.org/kids/home_page.html
Find out lots of information about Israel on this site.

www.woodlands-junior.kent.sch.uk/Homework/religion/jewish.htm
This web page will help you to learn more about Judaism.

Places to visit

If you go to Israel, these are some of the places you could visit:

The Dead Sea

You can read a book while floating here, or have a mud bath!

Masada National Park

Either take a cable car or walk along the Snake Path to the top of Masada, the ancient fortress that overlooks the Dead Sea.

The Dome of the Rock

The beautiful decoration of the Dome is well worth seeing.

Tower of David Museum

www.towerofdavid.org.il/English/General/Tower_of_David-Museum_of_the_History_of_Jerusalem

Visit the museum to learn about the history of Jerusalem.

Sea of Galilee

You can go for a boat ride to see the historic sites around the lake, or visit the Crusader Castle perched high above the Sea of Galilee.

Haifa

Haifa is built on a hill. You can go for a tram ride down the hillside, have a picnic in National Park Carmel, or go horseriding for the day.

Eilat

Eilat has beautiful beaches and lots of water sports. You can also visit Dolphin Reef to see the dolphins, or go on a camel trek.

Coral Beach Nature Reserve

This is Israel's only coral reef. You can see underwater gardens of coral and some beautifully coloured fish.

Topic tools

You can use these topic tools for your school projects. Trace the map onto a sheet of paper, using the thick black outline to guide you.

Israel's flag was adopted in 1948. The Star of David has long been an important symbol for Jews. The blue and white colours come from the Jewish prayer shawl. Copy the flag design and then colour in your picture. Make sure you use the right colours!

N

Jerusalem

Index

Abbas, Mahmoud 13
agriculture 16, 17, 20, 21
Arab–Israeli conflict 4, 8–13, 26
Arafat, Yasser 10, 11
area of Israel 36

Balfour Declaration 6
basketball 30
Ben-Gurion, David 8
bird species 18
bordering countries 4
British mandate 6

camping 31
climate 15
Coral Beach Nature Reserve 45
culture 27, 28–33
currency 36

daily life 16, 23, 24, 26
Dead Sea 14, 21, 24, 37
desalination 20
Dome of the Rock 5

earthquakes 15
economy 16–17, 36
education 18, 26
Eilat 45
employment 17
endangered animals 18
environmental issues 21
European Jews 6

falafel 33
film industry 30
food and meals 32–33

Gaza Strip 8, 11, 12, 22
global economic crisis 16
government 22

Haifa 45
Hamas 11, 12, 22
health 24
history 6–13, 40–41
Holocaust 6

immigration 10, 17, 34
imports and exports 36
industries 16, 17, 20, 21
infrastructure 22–27
internet access 25
Intifada 10
irrigation 20, 21
Israeli Jews 4, 8, 10, 12, 24, 27, 32

Jerusalem 4, 5, 7, 22, 23, 34

kibbutzim 14, 16
Knesset 22
Kosher laws 32

Lake Tiberias (Sea of Galilee) 14, 31
languages 4, 19, 23
life expectancy 36
literature 29

Maccabiah Games 30
Masada 44
media 25
medical care 24
Meir, Golda 39
mobile phones 25
mountains 15
music and dance 28
Muslims 4, 5, 27, 32

national anthem 38
national parks 20, 31, 44
national service 24, 26
natural resources 17
Negev Desert 15
Netanyahu, Benjamin 13

Orthodox Jews 31, 32
Oslo Accords 11

Palestinians 4, 6, 8, 10, 11, 12, 13, 17, 22, 24, 26, 27, 30, 32, 34
parliamentary democracy 22
peace talks 9, 10, 11, 12, 13, 34
plant species 19
PLO 10
pollution 21
population 4
public holidays 37

Rabin, Yitzhak 11
refugee camps 8, 34
religion 4, 31, 32
River Jordan 14

schools 26
settlements, Israeli 10, 12, 14, 24
Shabbat 32
Six Day War 9
spas 21, 24
sport 30
suicide bombers 11, 12, 34

Tel Aviv 28, 29, 34
theatres 28
tourism 34, 44–45
trading partners 4, 17

United Nations (UN) 8, 9

War of Independence 8
water conservation 20, 21
West Bank 8, 10, 11, 12, 22
Western Wall 35
wildlife 18–19
women 31

young people 18, 26–27, 31

Zionism 6, 8

Titles in the series

Title	ISBN
Afghanistan	978 1 406 22778 9
Algeria	978 1 406 23561 6
Australia	978 1 406 23533 3
Brazil	978 1 406 22785 7
Canada	978 1 406 23534 0
Chile	978 1 406 22786 4
China	978 1 406 23547 0
Costa Rica	978 1 406 22787 1
Cuba	978 1 406 22788 8
Czech Republic	978 1 406 22792 5
Egypt	978 1 406 23562 3
England	978 1 406 22799 4
Estonia	978 1 406 22793 2
France	978 1 406 22800 7
Germany	978 1 406 22801 4
Greece	978 1 406 23575 3
Haiti	978 1 406 22789 5
Hungary	978 1 406 22794 9
Iceland	978 1 406 23576 0
India	978 1 406 22779 6
Iran	978 1 406 22780 2
Iraq	978 1 406 22781 9
Ireland	978 1 406 23577 7
Israel	978 1 406 23535 7
Italy	978 1 406 22802 1
Japan	978 1 406 23548 7
Latvia	978 1 406 22795 6
Liberia	978 1 406 23563 0
Libya	978 1 406 23564 7
Lithuania	978 1 406 22796 3
Mexico	978 1 406 22790 1
Morocco	978 1 406 23565 4
New Zealand	978 1 406 23536 4
North Korea	978 1 406 23549 4
Pakistan	978 1 406 22782 6
Philippines	978 1 406 23550 0
Poland	978 1 406 22797 0
Portugal	978 1 406 23578 4
Russia	978 1 406 23579 1
Scotland	978 1 406 22803 8
South Africa	978 1 406 23537 1
South Korea	978 1 406 23551 7
Spain	978 1 406 23580 7
Tunisia	978 1 406 23566 1
United States of America	978 1 406 23538 8
Vietnam	978 1 406 23552 4
Wales	978 1 406 22804 5
Yemen	978 1 406 22783 3